HOW SHOULD I DEVELOP
HEAVENLY-MINDEDNESS
AND SPIRITUAL
CONVERSATION?

MAURICE ROBERTS

REFORMATION HERITAGE BOOKS
GRAND RAPIDS, MICHIGAN

*How Should I Develop Heavenly-Mindedness and
Spiritual Conversation?*
© 2018 by Maurice Roberts

Reformation Heritage Books
2965 Leonard St. NE
Grand Rapids, MI 49525
616-977-0889
orders@heritagebooks.org
www.heritagebooks.org

Printed in the United States of America
18 19 20 21 22 23/10 9 8 7 6 5 4 3 2 1

ISBN 978-1-60178-606-7
ISBN 978-1-60178-607-4 (e-pub)

*For additional Reformed literature, request a free book list from
Reformation Heritage Books at the above regular or e-mail address.*

HOW SHOULD I DEVELOP
HEAVENLY-MINDEDNESS AND SPIRITUAL CONVERSATION?

There are three ways that Christians should live in this world. First, we should live with a conscious understanding of God's existence and sovereignty. Second, we should live in grateful remembrance of all Christ has done for us as His people. Third, we should live with the steadfast conviction that God's daily dealings with us all are fully consistent with what He tells us in the Bible, which is His infallible Word.

All Christians are spiritual and heavenly-minded. But it should be the desire of all believers to grow, develop, and make progress in spirituality. In practice this means believers should see it as their great duty to become daily ever more conscious of God's sovereign control over all our life experiences. Also, we should strive to advance in our appreciation of all Christ's work for us. We should aim at seeking to interpret all God's daily dealings with us in the light of Holy Scripture.

Such is the wisdom of God's grace that He leaves room for our obedience in our spiritual growth and development. By this I mean that while His grace ensures salvation to all believers, we ourselves have the duty to exert our mind and soul to become as spiritual as we can.

To put it simply, we may say that our duty as believers is to become the most spiritual people we can be. That this is so is clear from the exhortations we are given in God's Word. "Grow in grace, and in the knowledge of our Lord and Saviour Jesus Christ" (2 Peter 3:18). "Seek those things which are above.... Set your affection on things above, not on things on the earth" (Col. 3:1–2). "Our conversation is in heaven" (Phil. 3:20).

WHAT IS HEAVENLY-MINDEDNESS?

Heavenly-mindedness in a Christian is a spiritual grace that begins at conversion and grows and develops with the passing of time. The crucial factor is not time, however, but the good and proper use to which Christians put their time. Let me emphasize that all spiritual progress is related to the degree of inward energy that believers put into their daily application of God's Word to the experiences of life.

A few practical examples may help to explain what I mean by our inward energy and our application of God's Word to our experience. Two Christians may experience a difficulty in life, yet one learns little from it while the other learns much. Two believers may have a disappointment. One learns to bless God for His wise providence, but the other seems to learn nothing. Two believers may make a bad decision in life. One pays little attention to the mistake; the other humbles himself in the dust before God and in the future learns to be far more conscientious than he was when he made his mistake.

Heavenly-mindedness is at the heart of the difference between the way one person learns from a situation and another does not. It should therefore be our great desire in life to exercise our soul in all situations so as to make the wisest choice. This is illustrated in the case of Abraham and Lot. When the moment arrived at which they had to part company, we read that Lot chose to live in the plain of Jordan and "pitched his tent toward Sodom" (Gen. 13:12). Both Abraham and Lot were true believers. But Abraham was more advanced than Lot in heavenly-mindedness. This must always be the formula in life: "Seek ye first the kingdom of God, and his righteousness" (Matt. 6:33). Sodom was anything but a place of righteousness.

Heavenly-mindedness is that instinct of the soul by which careful Christians choose not what appeals to their fancy but what they know to be consistent with the honor and glory of God. Solomon makes this point when he points a man to the wife he should choose: "Favour is deceitful, and beauty is vain: but a woman that feareth the LORD, she shall be praised" (Prov. 31:30). Woe to those who are hasty!

The index of people's spirituality is the degree to which they honor God in their mind. Worldly people's spirituality is nothing but zero. They have no place for God in all their thoughts. Hence the Bible declares: "The fool hath said in his heart, There is no God" (Ps. 14:1).

This attitude toward God is common. It is indicated in the theory of evolution and its invention of a big bang and millions of years, whereas God's Word clearly informs us that the world came into being by six wonderful acts of God's infinite power and wisdom. It is a test of the spirituality of our mind to read of God's works of creation. The snare is for our mind to waver between what God has revealed and what "science falsely so called" (1 Tim. 6:20) attempts to tell us in the name of scholarship and academic superiority.

The risk that we all face is that we are tempted to "dumb down" what God has told us by trying to accommodate Genesis 1–2 to fit in with university-type wisdom. This is done when people try to apologize for their faith in the Bible by referring to Genesis 1–2 as practical revelation not to be taken too seriously.

The consistent thing to do is to state that what God reveals in Scripture is not simply true—but absolutely true. It is the behavior of the less heavenly-minded to compromise the faith of the Bible by apologizing for what God has revealed. But our real duty is to state what is consistent with an infallible Bible. What God tells us may annoy some academic minds at Oxford, Cambridge, Harvard, and Yale. But the wisdom of this world is always "foolishness with God" (1 Cor. 3:19).

It must be said very clearly that the person who has not been regenerated by God's Holy Spirit cannot be expected to have any heavenly-mindedness. This is the plain teaching of the Lord Jesus Christ. The person who is not born again, says our Lord, "cannot see the kingdom of God" (John 3:3).

The apostle Paul echoes this teaching of our Lord when he tells us that there is a world of difference between the wisdom of men and the wisdom of God (1 Cor. 2:5–16). The things of God are "foolishness" (1 Cor. 2:14) to those who are strangers to the experience of the new birth. The meaning of this is that unbelievers live, very sadly, in a make-believe world. Tragically, they believe what is not true and dismiss as rubbish the sublime truths of God's Word: creation, providence, redemption, and eternal judgment. This is why unbelievers must be told of the gospel and of the regeneration that God alone can give to those who seek Him with all their heart. To die in unbelief is, for unbelievers, to discover after death that it would have been better for them if they had "never been born" (Mark 14:21).

Heavenly-mindedness, then, begins only after a person has been regenerated. This is how all the godly men and women of history came to be heavenly-minded. Paul, Luther, Calvin, the Puritans, the Covenanters, missionaries, and all who have excelled in spirituality, only got their heavenly mind when they experienced the new birth, which is the work of God's regenerating grace in the soul of a sinner. No one can thank him or herself for becoming spiritual. Heavenly-mindedness is the gift of God that people receive at their conversion. It enables them to believe what people cannot otherwise believe. This spiritual change is sent from heaven and it transforms a person from being a sinner to being a saint.

It is entirely possible for people, after conversion to Christ, to reverse completely what they believed before conversion. It is for this reason that a convert to Christ is in the Bible called a "new creature" (2 Cor. 5:17) and a "new man" (Eph. 2:15). God's work of regeneration enables sinners to believe what they utterly rejected before. Their eyes are now open to see that spiritual things, as set forth in the Bible, are real and true. The famous Thomas Chalmers of Scotland, who was wonderfully converted on his sickbed in 1810 or 1811, is a notable example of how God can give spiritual sight to those once spiritually blind.

The question to be faced then is this: How can we who are true believers in Christ develop and increase in heavenly-mindedness? The first thing we need to do is to be convinced that heavenly-mindedness is a great blessing to those who make progress in it. We recognize the difference between mediocrity and excellence in all walks of life, whether in sport, study, or any other area. Further, we realize that excellence in any area of life is achieved only by discipline and genuine effort.

So it is in this important matter of heavenly-mindedness. Believers must take appropriate steps to improve, both by correcting their own faults and by stirring themselves up to a higher level. So we now face the practical issue of how we may mature and progress in this excellent grace of heavenly-mindedness.

GROWING IN HEAVENLY-MINDEDNESS

Our first need is to make progress in godliness. The part of us that most needs to be improved is our spiritual and moral condition. Let us look at the spiritual side first. How may the true believer become more heavenly?

First, we need to take care to fill our mind and memory with Scripture and with right doctrine. Our doctrinal understanding controls our attitude to God—for better or for worse. We should seek to deepen our reverence and our fear of God. Time and again the Bible advises us to fear the Lord (e.g., Ps. 111:10; Prov. 1:7; 9:10). This fear is not a dread that drives us to hide from God. It is a deep respect for the glorious being of God who rules over the entire universe and to whom we are all accountable.

It is this devout attitude toward God that causes spiritual men and women to bow down in reverence and to adore Him with deep seriousness and delight. We must not think that this fear of God belonged only to the worship of Old Testament times. The apostle Paul tells us that he bowed "his knees unto the Father of our Lord Jesus Christ" (Eph. 3:14). The apostle John informs us that when he saw Christ in His glory, he "fell at his feet as dead" (Rev. 1:17).

Reverence is always in place when we think of the glorious being of the Triune God. It is essential to making progress in spirituality that we school ourselves to follow the example of the great apostles. Even Christ Himself, when in Gethsemane, "fell on his face" (Matt. 26:39) when He prayed to the Father. If Christ, who in His divine nature is equal to the Father, expressed His reverence in this way, how much more should we do so!

Heavenly-mindedness is very much helped by teaching ourselves to meditate on the Word of God. At night in bed, before we fall asleep, it is good to silently recite to ourselves texts of Scripture that give help, guidance, and comfort to the soul. Such texts could include the following: "Take therefore no thought for the morrow" (Matt. 6:34); "Our light affliction, which is but for a moment" (2 Cor. 4:17); and "Henceforth there is laid up for me a crown of righteousness" (2 Tim. 4:8).

As the soul is educated to look at life in the glass of Holy Scripture, it adjusts its attitude to time and eternity. We see, as we reflect on God's Word, how short and uncertain our earthly life is. We see too that only one thing matters above all: to be right with

God and, by faith in Christ, to be ready for death, judgment, and eternity.

There are five faculties of the soul, and if we are serious in our concern to grow in heavenly-mindedness, we must take account of these five faculties: mind, will, emotions, memory, and conscience. Every soul has these five elements, each of which needs to be taken into consideration as we strive for progress in godliness.

The faculties need to be cared for in the following ways. The *mind* must be fed with biblical truth, including both texts of Scripture and a system of good theology. The human *will* needs to be educated daily to conform in all things to the revealed will of God. The *emotions* need to be refreshed with the periodic enjoyment of those biblical experiences of which Scripture speaks: peace, joy, love, assurance, hope, and delight in God. The *memory* should be stored with Bible teaching. The *conscience* ought to be educated by believers to give us a warning conviction whenever we foolishly err or stray from what God commands us to do and be.

It follows from what we say here that conscientious believers must make it their daily and nightly duty to examine their own thoughts, deeds, and words. We all sin more than we realize. Our comfort is to be found in God's gracious promise: "If we confess our sins, he is faithful and just to forgive us our sins, and to cleanse us from all unrighteousness" (1 John 1:9). If we are serious in our pursuit of godliness and heavenliness, we must keep a close watch over all that we do, say, and think, so that we may confess our faults to God and enjoy His gracious pardon and peace.

THE PLACE OF THE MORAL LAW

One important and often neglected subject is God's moral law. In the Bible, there are three forms of law: two forms of law God gave in the Old Testament that do not apply to the believer in these New Testament times, and one form of law that was given in the period of the Old Testament is relevant to Christian believers today: the moral law. It is important to be clear on this subject of God's law so that we do not sin through ignorance.

The two forms of law that are no longer relevant to us are the ceremonial law and the judicial law. The ceremonial law consisted of the offering up of animal sacrifices and the sprinkling of blood to cleanse from sin in Old Testament times. This ceremonial law is now totally abolished since Christ, our Great High Priest, has offered up Himself on the cross to give us pardon and cleansing. Old Testament sacrifices were ordained by God for that period until Christ's work was complete. Today we must never reintroduce the ceremonial law in any way.

The judicial law, sometimes referred to as the civil law of the Old Testament, was God's law for Israel as a state. Israel was uniquely God's people in Old Testament times. God gave Israel laws that

The Place of the Moral Law

it was their duty to keep, as long as they were uniquely God's church on earth. But, on the day of Pentecost, the Holy Spirit, following the completion of Christ's work, was poured out, and now, in New Testament times, the nations are called to believe in the gospel of God. Hence we say that this form of law, the judicial law, has expired and does not bind our conscience.

The one form of law that remains is the moral law, which is forever binding on the consciences of all people. God originally wrote this moral law on the conscience of Adam. Later, in the time of Moses, God gave this moral law to us in the form of the Ten Commandments (Ex. 20:1–17). It is summed up briefly in this way: that we should love God with all our heart, soul, mind, and strength and also that we should love our neighbor as ourself. The Lord Jesus Christ affirms in His teaching that the moral law is still in effect (Matt. 22:37–40).

As Christians, we need to be clear about the place of the moral law in our life and worship if we seriously desire to become more heavenly-minded. Put simply, we say that we are not saved by keeping the Ten Commandments, but once we are saved those commandments become our daily, lifelong rule of duty.

Let me be clear on what this means. No one is saved by attempting to keep the moral law. We are justified and saved only by faith in Christ alone, whom God has given to be our Savior. But once we are justified and saved, it is our duty as Christians to carefully keep the moral law.

Christ makes this clear when He states in the Sermon on the Mount: "Think not that I am come to destroy the law" (Matt. 5:17). He clarifies what He means by stating two important things: the moral law will never be abolished (Matt. 5:18); and, the best Christians are those who keep the Ten Commandments; whereas the poorer Christians are those who break the Ten Commandments and teach others that they are free to break them (Matt. 5:19).

Here is a truth that, if we wish to make progress in spirituality and godliness, we dare not overlook. Justification is by faith in Christ alone, but the justified person's duty is to live with God's moral law as his or her rule of life. Too often this doctrine has been ignored or overlooked.

God is infinitely holy, and He requires of His rational creatures that they obey His commandments. If they obey His commands, He will bless them. If they do not obey, they will suffer loss. This means that true Christians who are careless about keeping the Ten Commandments will suffer loss. What loss is this?

They will not lose their souls because they are sinners saved by grace, but they will lose other important things. What are these things? They will *lose comfort*. They will *lose many blessings* in life. They will *not make as much progress* in heavenly-mindedness as they ought to make. They may *lose assurance* of their salvation. They will lose some of the *eternal reward* that they would have gotten in the great day of judgment. Christ tells us, "He shall be called the least in the kingdom of heaven" (Matt. 5:19a). These words of Christ are extremely relevant to the question: How should I develop heavenly-mindedness? Let the words of our blessed Lord ring in our ears: "Whosoever shall do and teach them [the Ten Commandments], the same shall be called great in the kingdom of heaven" (Matt. 5:19b).

It is all too easy for Christians who have not faced up to the doctrine of the moral law as their rule of life to cry, "But surely this is legalism!" How are we to answer this charge? We answer it like this: Legalism is the false gospel which teaches that sinners are saved by their good works; but we do not teach that. We teach that sinners are saved only by faith in Christ. But when sinners are saved, their duty is to live a life of obedience to the God who, by grace, has saved them. The form this obedience ought to take is obedience to God's moral law, the Ten Commandments.

There are, let it be remembered, two very different errors that we must never confuse. These are legalism and antinomianism. Legalism teaches that sinners may be saved by their own good works. This is false! Sinners are saved only by faith in Jesus Christ, who died on the cross for those who believe. But the other error is to let saved sinners imagine that they have no rule of duty that God requires them to live by. Put simply, the issues are these. We are justified by faith alone, but we are sanctified by faith together with works. The true believer, now saved, wants to know: "How can I live so as to glorify and honor my beloved Savior?" To this question we answer: "We glorify God and Christ by living obediently and keeping the Ten Commandments." How do we prove this to be true? By the words of our Savior: "He that hath my commandments and keepeth them, he it is that loveth me" (John 14:21). Again, our Savior says: "If a man love me, he will keep my words" (John 14:23).

The way to grow in holiness and in heavenly-mindedness is made clear in God's Word. The apostle John states, "Hereby we do know that we know him [God], if we keep his commandments" (1 John 2:3). Keeping God's moral law is the way true believers express their love for God. This supremely important truth is stated again clearly on the last page of Holy Scripture: "Blessed are they that do his commandments" (Rev. 22:14).

As a generation we have allowed this doctrine of the moral law as the believer's rule of life to fade into the background. It has been crowded out of people's minds by other things: singing unbiblical lyrics in church, speaking in tongues, and so on. It is time for us, however, to get back to this doctrine so very much emphasized by the Puritans, that the moral law "doth for ever bind all, as well justified persons as others, to the obedience thereof" (Westminster Confession of Faith, chapter 19).

The way to become more spiritual, holy, and heavenly involves the believer in the duty of striving to keep God's Commandments carefully every day of his or her life. We dare not allow our modern religious culture, with its love of loud music and excessive self-confidence, to blind us to the words of our blessed Savior: "He that hath my commandments and keepeth them, he it is that loveth me" (John 14:21).

The Ten Commandments are an important means by which we should watch over and examine our life from hour to hour and from day to day. It is true that believers are not now, since their conversion to Christ, under the moral law as a covenant. Yet the Ten Commandments are important as a means of detecting our own moral weaknesses.

It is profitable to review our own life regularly in the light of each of the Ten Commandments. We should have no God but the true God only. But have I loved and glorified Him *today* as He deserves? Since I may not make any image of God, I may not allow any pictures of Jesus to be put up on the wall of my house because Jesus is a person of the Godhead. God is a Trinity, and therefore I may not support any religious movement that is not Trinitarian in its confession.

The third commandment says never to take God's name in vain. But have I used any minced oaths in conversation? We must not say "Gee!" for this is possibly a minced form of Jesus. We must not say "Gosh!" for this is a minced form of God. These are examples of how we must apply the third commandment to every area of our life, thought, and speech.

The fourth commandment requires us to keep the Sabbath day holy. In the Old Testament era, this day was the seventh day of the week. But since Christ's resurrection, it is the first day. We should therefore arrange our life so as to do no secular work on this day but to spend the whole day in the public and private exercises of God's worship, except for works of necessity and mercy.

The fifth commandment requires us to respect our parents. By implication it further requires us to respect all who are above us in authority, such as teachers, law enforcement workers, and government officials. It is lawful for us to criticize the policies of our government leaders. But we should do so only in a respectful way.

The Ten Commandments need to be kept not only in an outward way but also in our thoughts. This is made clear in the Sermon on the Mount, where Christ tells us that to be angry without a cause is breaking the commandment not to kill (Matt. 5:21–22). Similarly, to look lustfully on a woman is, in God's judgment, to commit a form of adultery (Matt. 5:27–28).

In light of these examples, which Christ explains in the Sermon on the Mount, we all need to keep a careful watch over our inward thoughts, moods, and imaginations. God is always watching how we behave. But, more importantly, He is always watching how we think as well as what we do.

Progressive sanctification is the technical term for growth in grace in the life of the true Christian. It is an important part of our Christian life. More than that, it is a demanding part of the Christian life. It requires us to be on the watch all the time, making sure that our motives and our secret thoughts are in conformity with God's law. If at any time we recognize that we have a bad motive or a sinful thought, we need to pause and secretly confess our guilt to God. Mercifully, God has promised to pardon us as believers. But we must be constantly on the watch.

SPIRITUAL CONVERSATION

So far we have been looking at the subject of heavenly-mindedness and how, as Christians, we may strive to improve in this aspect of our life. We come now, finally, to look at the subject of how, as believers, we may improve in spiritual conversation. It is important that we should discipline ourselves to talk about spiritual and biblical subjects, and it is good for us to do so. It may lead to the good of those who hear us speak about the things of God.

John Bunyan, the renowned Puritan author whose books have been translated into many languages, tells us in his *Grace Abounding to the Chief of Sinners* that, as a young man, he was helped by the godly conversation of "three or four poor women sitting at a door in the sun." They referred, said Bunyan, to "their soul's miserable state by nature" and how "God had visited their souls with His love in the Lord Jesus." The effect, says Bunyan, was that he felt his heart "begin to shake." He now began to see the importance of the new birth. This experience was life-changing for Bunyan. It led to his writing sixty books in sixty years—books that have been so important to the spiritual life of others that we cannot begin to calculate how much good they have done.

This experience of the author of the great *Pilgrim's Progress* ought to stir us up, if we have experienced the new birth, to cultivate spiritual conversation. Who can know the good that it might do to those who hear our godly talk?

Let us ask ourselves why more Christians seem not to excel in spiritual conversation. Sometimes it is because they are rather shy and do not want to tell others what they have laid up in the secret place of their own heart. But this can be a mistake. Provided we always speak humbly and always aim to honor God for His love to us in Christ, we should be prepared to tell others, who are also God's people, about our experiences of God's grace. What might we tell them? We might tell them a little about our ignorance of God before our conversion and then, at greater length, tell them how God opened our heart and gave us the wonderful experience of forgiveness and assurance of His love.

As we grow in experience, we need to assess the level of understanding of the people in our religious company. Our level of spiritual talk needs to be appropriate for the level of our hearers' understanding. We ought never to engage in spiritual conversation to draw attention to ourselves or to our gifts and abilities. Our supreme concern is to help the ignorant to see their need of Christ. And we desire to discuss with young believers subjects that will be a means of their growing in grace and understanding of the Bible.

The following guidelines will be a help to those who wish to promote religious conversation:

- Urge people on the Lord's Day to engage one another to talk only about biblical subjects.

- After attending a sermon it is good to stir others up by mentioning some point which the preacher made. You might ask, for example, "What did the preacher say about the implications of the gospel for our daily lives in 1 Corinthians 15?"

- Ask a friend what he or she has been reading in his or her personal devotions.

- Ask a friend what book of the Bible he or she is reading in family worship.

- Begin a conversation with, "Let me tell you the text that was blessed to me at my conversion. What text helped you?"

- You could ask, "What text do you want on your gravestone? I want mine to be, 'I know that my Redeemer liveth!'"

- You might ask a child, "How did Adam and Eve sin in the garden of Eden? What was God's solution to their problem?"

- You might ask an elderly Christian, "What will you say to Christ when you first see Him?"

- You could ask a Christian lacking assurance, "What promises of God give you most comfort?"

- In a Bible study, the leader could invite conversation by asking, "What text of Scripture shall we discuss so as to get a better understanding of it?"

It is a wonderful encouragement to remember that God delights in spiritual conversation. If there are those who doubt it, let them read what sacred Scripture tells us on the subject:

Then they that feared the LORD spake often one to another: and the LORD hearkened, and heard it, and a book of remembrance was written before him for them that feared the LORD, and that thought upon his name. And they shall be mine, saith the LORD of hosts, in that day when I make up my jewels; and I will spare them, as a man spareth his own son that serveth him. Then shall ye return, and discern between the righteous and the wicked, between him that serveth God and him that serveth him not. (Mal. 3:16–18)

CONCLUSION

We have looked at two valuable aspects of Christian godliness: heavenly-mindedness and spiritual conversation. These two subjects are important for every true Christian to think about. The essential duty of every believer is to seek to live to the glory of God and to be as perfect a child of God as possible.

The more we grow in heavenly-mindedness, the more we will shine as lights in this dark world. And the more we aim to promote God-honoring conversation, the more we will be seen to walk in the steps of our Master Jesus Christ, of whom it was truly said, "No man ever spake like this man" (John 7:46).